Product Management 101

The Art and Science of Product Management

Rathnakumar Udayakumar

www.rathnakumar.com

Copyright Page

Copyright © 2023 by Rathnakumar Udayakumar All rights reserved. No part of this book may be reproduced, stored in a retrieval system, or transmitted in any form or by any means, electronic, mechanical, photocopying, recording, or otherwise, without the prior written permission of the publisher.

This eBook is licensed for your personal use only. It may not be re-sold or given away to other people. If you would like to share this book with another person, please purchase an additional copy for each recipient. If you are reading this book and did not purchase it, or it was not purchased for your use only, then please return it to your favorite eBook retailer and purchase your own copy. Thank you for respecting the demanding work of this author.

Disclaimer: The information provided in this eBook is for general informational purposes only. The author and publisher make no representations or warranties of any kind, express or implied, about the completeness, accuracy, reliability, suitability, or availability with respect to the eBook or the information, products, services, or related graphics contained in the eBook for any purpose. Any reliance you place on such information is therefore strictly at your own risk.

Table of Contents

Introduction to Product Management 5
Introduction to Product Development 7
Ideas and User Needs 10
Competitive and Market Analysis 11
Customer Development 13
Designing and Running Experiments: 15
Conceptualizing the Solution 20
Metrics for Product Managers: 22
Building the Product 24
Working with People and Stakeholders 27
What You Should Do to Prepare Yourself for the Job 29
How to Look for a Job in Product Management 31
How to Get a Job in Product Management 33
After You've Got the Job the first things to do 37

Introduction

Product Management

Welcome to the world of Product Management! Whether you are new to the field or have been working in it for a while, this eBook is designed to provide you with an in-depth understanding of the key concepts and principles of product management. Product management is the process of bringing a product to market and overseeing its success. It involves identifying customer needs, developing a product strategy, and working closely with cross-functional teams to bring the product to life.

In this eBook, you will learn about the role of the product manager, the product development process, and the skills and tools needed to be successful in this field. You will also learn about best practices in product management, and how to use data and customer feedback to make informed decisions. We will also discuss the challenges and opportunities of product management in today's fast-paced and rapidly changing business environment.

This eBook is designed for anyone who wants to learn more about product management, whether you are a student, a professional, or an entrepreneur. It is a comprehensive guide that will provide you with a solid foundation in product management and give you the tools you need to be successful in this field.

So, let us dive in and explore the exciting world of product management together!

Introduction to Product Management

What is a product manager?

A product manager is responsible for the strategy, development, and marketing of a company's products. They work with cross-functional teams, including engineers, designers, salespeople, and marketers, to ensure that the product meets the needs of customers and the business. They also oversee the entire lifecycle of a product, from ideation to launch and beyond.

What is a product?

A product is a good or service that is created to meet a customer's needs or wants. It can be physical, such as a smartphone, or digital, such as a mobile app. Products can be simple or complex, and they can serve a variety of purposes, from entertainment to productivity to health and wellness.

Three type of product manager roles

There are several types of product manager roles, including:

- **Technical Product Manager:** This type of product manager has a strong technical background and is responsible for overseeing the development of complex products or software.

- **Business Product Manager:** This type of product manager focuses on the financial and strategic aspects of product development, such as pricing, positioning, and go-to-market strategies.

- **UX/Product Design Product Manager:** This type of product manager is responsible for ensuring that the product's user experience is intuitive, easy to use, and visually appealing.

How to think about the type of PM you want to be

When thinking about the type of product manager you want to be, it is important to consider your strengths and interests. If you have a technical background and enjoy working with engineers, a technical product manager role may be a good fit. If you have a background in business or marketing and enjoy strategic planning, a business product manager role may be more up your alley. Finally, if you have a background in design and enjoy creating user-friendly products, a UX/product design manager role may be the right fit.

Product vs Project management

Product management focuses on the strategy and development of a product, while project management focuses on the execution of a project. Product managers are responsible for the big picture, including the product's vision, roadmap, and customer needs, while project managers are responsible for the day-to-day management of tasks and timelines to ensure the project is completed on time and within budget.

A day in the life of a product manager

A day in the life of a product manager can vary depending on the company and the product they are working on. However, a typical day might involve:

- Reviewing customer feedback and market trends to inform product strategy.

- Meeting with cross-functional teams, such as engineers and designers, to discuss product development and design.
- Analyzing data and metrics to measure the success of the product.
- Developing a roadmap for future product releases
- Working with marketing and sales teams to create a go-to-market strategy for the product.
- Communicating with stakeholders, such as executives or investors, to update them on the product's progress.

Why product management is awesome.

Product management is a dynamic and exciting role that allows you to work on innovative products that can impact people's lives. It requires a combination of technical, business, and creative skills, which means there is always something new to learn. Additionally, product managers get to work with a variety of teams, from engineers to marketers to designers, which can be both challenging and rewarding. Finally, product management is a highly in-demand field with competitive salaries and room for growth.

Introduction to Product Development

The Four Major Phases of the Product Lifecycle:

The product lifecycle is the process through which a product goes from the idea stage to the end of its life. There are four major phases of the product lifecycle: introduction, growth, maturity, and decline.

Introduction:

In this phase, the product is first introduced to the market. The company invests heavily in advertising and promotion to create awareness and generate demand. The product is usually in limited supply, and the company is still testing the market. For example, when Apple launched the first iPhone in 2007, it was in the introduction phase.

Growth:

In the growth phase, the product starts gaining traction, and sales begin to increase. The company may start expanding the product line or introducing new features. In the growth phase, the company needs to focus on quality control and customer satisfaction. An example of a product in the growth phase is the Tesla Model S, which has seen an increase in sales and popularity over the years.

Maturity:
The maturity phase is when the product has reached its maximum potential and sales start to level off. The company may start to face competition from other products or companies and may need to introduce new features to keep up. A good example of a product in the maturity phase is the Toyota Prius, which has been in the market for over 20 years.

Decline:

In the decline phase, sales start to decline, and the company may need to phase out the product or find new ways to market it. An example of a product in the decline phase is the Blackberry smartphone, which was once a popular product but lost out to competition from Apple and Android phones.

Product Lifecycle Phases: Real-World Examples

Real-world examples of products in distinct phases of the product lifecycle are:

- Introduction: Apple Air tag
- Growth: Amazon Echo
- Maturity: Honda Civic
- Decline: Flip Video Camera

Product Development Process:

The product development process is the process through which a company creates new products or improves existing products. The process involves several stages, including idea generation, product design, testing, and launch. The product development process requires collaboration between different departments, including engineering, design, marketing, and sales.

Getting Deeper into the Product Development Process:

Getting deeper into the product development process involves understanding the various stages and the various activities that take place in each stage. The stages of the product development process include ideation, concept development, product design, testing, and launch. The process involves identifying customer needs, creating a product roadmap, conducting market research, and building a prototype. Each stage requires a separate set of skills and expertise.

What is Lean Product Development?

Lean Product Development is a methodology that focuses on reducing waste and increasing efficiency in the product development process. It involves creating a culture of continuous improvement, optimizing processes, and prioritizing customer needs. Lean Product Development also emphasizes the importance of cross-functional collaboration and creating a feedback loop between different departments.

What is Agile?

Agile is a project management methodology that emphasizes flexibility, collaboration, and customer feedback. It involves breaking down projects into small, manageable chunks called sprints and constantly iterating and adapting based on feedback. Agile is popular in software development but can be applied to other industries as well.

What is Scrum and How Does it Work?

Scrum is a specific framework of Agile that is used for managing software development projects. It involves a cross-functional team that works together to deliver a product incrementally. The team works in sprints, with a set amount of work to be completed in each sprint. The team meets regularly to review progress and adapt the plan as needed.

What is Kanban and How Does it Work?

Kanban is a project management methodology that emphasizes visualizing work, limiting work in progress, and continuously delivering small batches of work. It involves using a visual board, typically a whiteboard or an online tool, to track the progress of work items. Each item is represented by a card that moves through various stages of the process, from "to do" to "in progress" to "done." The goal is to optimize the flow of work and identify and eliminate bottlenecks in the process.

What is Waterfall Development?

Waterfall development is a traditional project management methodology that emphasizes completing each phase of a project before moving on to the next phase. The phases typically include requirements gathering, design, development, testing, and deployment. The waterfall approach is sequential, with little room for changes or iterations once a phase is complete. It is often used in industries such as construction or manufacturing, where the requirements are well-defined, and the product is fixed.

Real-World Examples of Waterfall and Agile:

Real-world examples of products developed using Waterfall and Agile methodologies are:

- Waterfall: Boeing 747 aircraft, the development of the Boeing 747 aircraft followed the Waterfall methodology, with each phase of the project completed before moving on to the next phase.

- Agile: Spotify music streaming service, the development of the Spotify music streaming service, on the other hand, follows the Agile methodology, with continuous iterations and adaptations based on customer feedback.

Ideas and User Needs

As a product manager, one of your main responsibilities is to identify and meet the needs of your users or customers. To do that, you need to have a clear understanding of their needs and pain points. This involves a deep dive into their behaviors, preferences, and challenges. It also requires you to generate and evaluate ideas that can address their needs.

Where Ideas Come from as a PM and Getting Real User Needs:

Ideas can come from a variety of sources, such as market research, competitive analysis, user feedback, and internal brainstorming sessions. As a product manager, you need to be open to innovative ideas and constantly explore new possibilities. You can also leverage the creativity and expertise of your team to generate and evaluate innovative ideas.
Identifying the real user needs requires empathy, active listening, and an open mind. It involves talking to users, observing their behaviors, and analyzing their feedback. You need to be able to distill their pain points into clear and actionable insights that can guide the product development process.

Users vs. Customers:

It is important to differentiate between users and customers. While users are the people who use your product, customers are the people who pay for it. The needs and goals of these two groups may not always align, and it is your job as a product manager to balance their needs and create a product that serves both groups. Understanding the nuances of user and customer needs can help you make informed decisions and create a product that meets the needs of both groups.

Competitive and Market Analysis

Market Research: Sizing the Market:

Before launching a new product or feature, it is essential to understand the size and potential of the market you are entering. Market research can help you evaluate the market size, growth rate, customer segments, and other critical factors that can affect the success of your product.

Introduction to Finding Competitors:

To create a successful product, you need to understand your competition. This involves identifying and analyzing direct, indirect, and potential competitors in your market. As a product manager, you should be constantly monitoring the competitive landscape to identify inexperienced players and emerging trends.

Direct, Indirect, and Potential Competitors and their Impact:

- Direct competitors are companies that offer the same or related products as your company.
- Indirect competitors offer comparable products or services that solve the same problem but may be targeted at a different market or customer segment.
- Potential competitors are companies that may enter your market in the future. Understanding the impact of these competitors on your product strategy can help you make informed decisions about pricing, marketing, and feature development.

The Five Criteria for Understanding Competitors:

The five criteria for understanding competitors are their strengths and weaknesses, their business models, their marketing strategies, their target customers, and their pricing strategies. By analyzing these factors, you can gain a better understanding of your competition and how to differentiate your product in the market.

The Last Three Criteria for Understanding Competitors:

The last three criteria for understanding competitors are their product features, their user experience, and their customer support. By evaluating these factors, you can identify opportunities for improvement in your own product and create a better overall user experience.

Monitor Competitors:

To stay ahead of the competition, it is important to continuously monitor their activities and stay up to date on industry trends. This can involve tracking their product releases, marketing campaigns, and social media activity.

What is a Feature Table?

A feature table is a tool that compares the features of your product to those of your competitors. It allows you to visualize how your product stacks up against the competition and identify areas for improvement.

Put Together a Feature Table:

To create a feature table, you should list the key features of your product and those of your competitors. You can then rate each feature based on its importance to your target customers and its effectiveness in addressing their needs.

Practice Building a Feature Table:

To practice building a feature table, you can choose a product category and list out the features of your product and those of your competitors. You can then rate each feature and use the information to identify opportunities for improvement.

What Do We Ultimately Care About as Product Managers?

As product managers, we care about creating a successful product that meets the needs of our customers and generates revenue for our company. This requires a deep understanding of our customers, competition, and market trends. By gathering and analyzing this information, we can make informed decisions about feature development, pricing, and marketing that drive the success of our product.

Customer Development

Customer development is a process that involves interacting with customers to validate assumptions about a product or service. It is an essential part of product management that allows you to understand your customers' needs and preferences.

The Four Types of Customer Interviews:

The four types of customer interviews are problem discovery interviews, solution discovery interviews, validation interviews, and usability testing. Each type of interview serves a different purpose and can help you gather valuable insights from your customers.

Key Differences in Customer Development:

Customer development is different from traditional market research in that it involves direct interaction with customers. This allows you to get firsthand feedback on your product or service and build a deeper understanding of your customers' needs.

Who You Should Talk To:

When conducting customer interviews, it is important to talk to the right people. You should target customers who are representative of your target market and have experience with your product or service.

How to Find Interviewees Externally:

There are several ways to find interviewees externally, including social media, industry events, and customer referrals. You can also use online survey tools to gather feedback from a larger audience.

How to Find Interviewees Internally:

If you are working for a company that already has customers, you can reach out to your customer support or sales team to identify potential interviewees. You can also leverage your personal network to find people who are willing to participate in interviews.

How to Get Them to Talk:

To get interviewees to talk to, you need to make them feel comfortable and valued. Be transparent about the purpose of the interview, listen actively, and show empathy for their experiences and challenges.

Practice Writing Emails:

Crafting an effective email is an essential part of the customer development process. To practice writing emails, you can start by identifying potential interviewees and drafting a brief message that explains the purpose of the interview and the benefits of participating.

How to Run a Customer Interview Correctly:

Running a successful customer interview requires careful planning and preparation. You should develop a list of open-ended questions that allow the interviewee to provide detailed and meaningful feedback. It is also important to create a comfortable and safe environment where the interviewee feels free to share their honest thoughts and opinions.

Good Questions, Bad Questions:

Good questions are open-ended, non-leading, and focused on the customer's experience and perspective. Bad questions are closed-ended, leading, and focused on validating assumptions or gathering specific data points.

Build User Personas off Your Interviews:

User personas are fictional representations of your ideal customer. They are based on real-world data and can help you make informed decisions about product development and marketing. By analyzing the data gathered from customer interviews, you can build detailed user personas that capture the needs, preferences, and behaviors of your target market.

Real-World Examples of User Persona:

Real-world examples of user personas include "Busy Bob," "Frugal Frank," and "Tech-Savvy Tina." These personas are based on data gathered from customer interviews and are used to inform product development and marketing strategies.

The Product Manager and the Data Diet:

The data diet is a metaphor for the process of collecting and analyzing customer data to inform product decisions. As a product manager, you should strive to maintain a healthy data diet by regularly gathering and analyzing data and using it to make informed decisions about your product.

Designing and Running Experiments:

Designing and Running Experiments:

One of the fundamental principles of product management is testing assumptions through experimentation. This involves designing and running an MVP, or Minimum Viable Product, which is a scaled-down version of the product that tests key assumptions with minimal investment. In this chapter, we will explore the process of designing and running experiments for your product.

What is an MVP?

An MVP is a product or service with the minimum set of features required to validate key assumptions about the market, user needs, and the product itself. It allows you to test the waters before investing significant resources into a full-fledged product launch. The MVP can be anything from a basic landing page to a physical prototype if it can validate assumptions.

What do product managers think about MVPs?

Product managers think of MVPs as a tool for validating assumptions about the product and the market. They focus on creating an MVP that can answer the most important questions about the product in the simplest way possible. An MVP should be designed to test the riskiest assumptions, with the goal of creating a product that people want and are willing to pay for.

Seven steps to running an MVP experiment:

1. **Identify your assumptions:** Make a list of all the assumptions you are making about your product, market, and users.

2. **Find the riskiest assumption of them all:** Identify the most important assumption you are making about your product, which will determine the success or failure of your product.

3. **Make decisions:** The risk/difficulty square: Decide which assumptions to test based on their level of risk and difficulty.

4. **What is a hypothesis:** A hypothesis is a statement that can be tested to determine its validity. It should be specific, measurable, and tied to a specific assumption.

5. **Put together a hypothesis:** Use the assumptions you have identified to create a hypothesis that can be tested through an MVP.

6. **What is the minimum criterion for success:** Define the minimum criterion for success or the minimum acceptable outcome of the experiment.

7. **Evaluate results and learn from them:** Analyze the results of the MVP experiment and use the insights gained to inform future product development.

MVP techniques: Emails, shadows, 404, and coming soon.

There are several techniques for creating an MVP, including emails, shadows, 404, and coming soon pages. These techniques involve creating a simple and inexpensive version of the product or service to validate key assumptions. Let us take a closer look at these techniques.

Email-based MVPs: These involve sending an email to potential customers to gauge their interest in the product or service. The email can include a description of the product and a call to action, such as signing up for a newsletter or filling out a survey.

Shadow buttons: This technique involves adding a button to a website that seems functional but does not do anything. This allows you to measure interest in a particular feature before investing in its development.

404 and coming soon MVPs: These involve creating a simple landing page that indicates the product is either not yet available or is coming soon. This allows you to gauge interest in the product without investing significant resources.

Explainer videos: These involve creating a short video that explains the product or service to potential customers. This can be used to test whether the product is easy to understand and whether there is demand for it.

Piecemeal MVPs: These involve creating a simple version of the product or service that only includes one or two features. This allows you to test whether the core value proposition is compelling to customers.

Concierge service MVPs: These involve manually providing the service to customers as if it were fully automated. This allows you to test the demand for the service and whether customers are willing to pay for it.

How do big companies think about MVP experiments, evaluating results, and learning from them?

Big companies approach MVP experiments differently than startups because they have more resources, larger user bases, and established brand recognition. Big companies use MVP experiments to test new features or products, improve existing products, and learn from their customers.

One approach that big companies use is to run small-scale experiments with a select group of customers or users. They use A/B testing, in which they randomly assign users to two different versions of a product or feature and track how they perform. This approach allows them to evaluate the impact of a particular change and decide whether to proceed with a full-scale rollout.

Another approach is to run pilot programs, in which they test a product or feature with a small group of customers in a specific market or region. This approach allows them to gather feedback from customers and refine the product before rolling it out to a larger audience.

After running an MVP experiment, big companies use data analysis to evaluate the results and learn from them. They look at metrics such as user engagement, retention, and revenue to determine the success of the experiment. They also gather feedback from users through surveys, focus groups, or other forms of user research.

Based on the results of the experiment, big companies may decide to proceed with a full-scale rollout, make changes to the product, or even scrap the idea entirely. They use what they learn from the experiment to inform future product development and decision-making.

In summary, big companies use MVP experiments to test new products and features, improve existing products, and learn from their customers. They approach MVP experiments with a more extensive user base and more resources than startups, and they use data analysis and user feedback to evaluate the results and make informed decisions.

Conceptualizing the Solution

When it comes to product development, one of the first steps is to conceptualize the solution. This involves identifying a problem and brainstorming potential solutions to that problem. Once you have a potential solution in mind, you will need to begin creating a plan for how that solution will be executed. This can involve creating wireframes, mockups, and prototypes, which we will cover in more detail below.

Introduction to Wireframing:

Wireframing is a crucial step in the product development process. It involves creating a basic visual representation of what the final product will look like. Wireframes are typically created using simple shapes and boxes, and they can help you to identify potential design issues before investing too much time and resources into the product.

Wireframe, Mockup, Prototype:

Wireframes, mockups, and prototypes are all important steps in the product development process. Wireframes are basic visual representations of the product, while mockups are more detailed visual representations that show what the final product will look like. Prototypes are functional versions of the product that can be tested by users to identify potential issues.

Jump into Sketching:

Sketching is an important part of the wireframing process. It allows you to sketch out ideas quickly and easily for the product without investing too much time or resources. Sketching can be done using pen and paper or using digital tools such as Sketch or Figma.

Sketching out a mobile app:

When it comes to sketching out a mobile app, there are several things to keep in mind. You will need to consider the user interface, the user experience, and the overall flow of the app. It is important to keep things simple and intuitive, and to focus on the most key features of the app.

Using POP:

POP is a digital tool that allows you to turn your sketches into a functional prototype. It is a great tool for quickly testing out ideas and identifying potential issues with the product. With POP, you can link your sketches together to create a basic prototype that can be tested by users.

Intro to Balsamiq:

Balsamiq is another digital tool that can be used for wireframing and prototyping. It allows you to create detailed mockups of your product, and it includes a library of pre-made components that can be used to speed up the design process. Balsamiq is a great tool for creating more detailed designs that can be used to communicate your vision to stakeholders.

Building YouTube in Balsamiq:

Building YouTube in Balsamiq can be a great exercise for anyone looking to improve their wireframing and prototyping skills. By creating a mockup of a complex product like YouTube, you will be forced to think about the product in a more detailed way, which can help you to identify potential issues and produce more creative solutions. Additionally, creating a mockup of a well-known product like YouTube can be a wonderful way to highlight your skills to potential employers or clients.

Metrics for Product Managers:

Metrics for Product Managers: Defining Success and Measuring Results:

Metrics is a valuable tool for product managers to measure the success of their product and make data-driven decisions. To pick the right metrics, it is important to understand what they are and how they can be used.

Introduction to Metrics:

Metrics are simply a way of measuring and tracking data. They can be used to track a wide range of different things, from user engagement to revenue. Metrics are a crucial tool for product managers because they can help you to understand how your product is performing and identify areas for improvement.

Real-life examples of Metrics:

There are many diverse types of metrics that product managers might use to track the success of their product. Some examples might include user engagement metrics such as time spent on the product, conversion metrics such as signups or purchases, or revenue metrics such as total sales or customer lifetime value.

Metrics of all kinds:

There are many diverse types of metrics that product managers might use, depending on the goals of their product. Some metrics might be more focused on user engagement, while others might be more focused on revenue or customer satisfaction. It is important to pick the right metrics for your product and your goals.

How to pick good metrics:

When picking metrics, it is important to consider your product goals and what you are trying to achieve. You will want to pick metrics that are relevant to your product and that can help you to make data-driven decisions. It is also important to pick metrics that are measurable and can be tracked consistently over time.

Using the HEART Metrics Framework: Part 1:

The HEART metrics framework is a popular tool for product managers to measure the user experience of their product. HEART stands for Happiness, Engagement, Adoption, Retention, and Task Success. Each of these metrics can be used to measure various aspects of the user experience and identify areas for improvement

Using the HEART Metrics Framework: Part 2:

To use the HEART metrics framework effectively, it is important to understand how to measure each of the different metrics. For example, happiness might be measured using customer surveys, while engagement might be measured using time spent on the product. By tracking these metrics over time, product managers can identify areas for improvement and make data-driven decisions.

Using the AARRR (Pirate) Metrics Framework:

The AARRR metrics framework is another popular tool for product managers to track the success of their products. AARRR stands for Acquisition, Activation, Retention, Revenue, and Referral. Each of these metrics can be used to track various stages of the customer journey, from acquisition to referral.

Tracking Your Metrics in Practice:

Once you have picked the right metrics for your product and goals, it is important to track them consistently over time. This can involve setting up a dashboard to track your metrics, or regularly reviewing and analyzing your data to identify areas for improvement. By using data to make decisions, product managers can make more informed decisions and create a better product for their users.

Building the Product

Building the Product: Project Management for PMs:

Product managers often play a critical role in project management, ensuring that their team is working efficiently and effectively to build an excellent product. To do this, they need to have a good understanding of how to manage projects, and how to work with their team to set goals and priorities.

Introduction to Epics:

An epic is a large, high-level feature or project that is broken down into smaller, more manageable tasks. Epics are often used to organize a product roadmap and ensure that the team is working towards a common goal. By breaking a large project into smaller epics, product managers can help their team to stay focused and on track.

Let us Get into Epic Specs:

Once you have identified an epic, the next step is to create a specification or plan for how to implement it. This might include things like defining the scope of the epic, setting goals or milestones, and identifying any dependencies or risks. Epic specs are important because they help to ensure that everyone on the team has a clear understanding of what needs to be done and what the result should look like.

User Stories and Acceptance Criteria:

User stories are a way of defining specific features or functionality within an epic. User stories typically start with the phrase "As a user, I want to..." and describe a specific goal or need that the user has. Acceptance criteria define how the user story should be implemented and tested. User stories and acceptance criteria are important because they help to ensure that the team is working towards a common goal and that everyone has a clear understanding of what needs to be done.

Real-life Examples of Epics, Specs, User Stories, and the Backlog:

In practice, epics, specs, user stories, and the backlog are often used in tandem to manage projects and ensure that the team is working efficiently. For example, a product manager might start by identifying an epic, then work with the team to create a spec, define user stories and acceptance criteria, and prioritize the work in the backlog. This can help to ensure that everyone on the team is working towards a common goal and that progress is being made toward that goal.

Estimations and Velocity:

Estimations and velocity are important tools for project management because they help to ensure that the team is making progress and meeting deadlines. Estimations involve assigning time estimates to specific tasks or user stories, while velocity is a measure of how quickly the team can complete work. By tracking velocity and estimations, product managers can identify areas where the team might be falling behind or where additional resources might be needed.

Road mapping:

A roadmap is a high-level plan that outlines the goals and priorities for a product over a set of time. Road mapping is a crucial tool for product managers because it helps to ensure that everyone on the team is working towards a common goal and that progress is being made towards that goal. By setting goals and priorities on a roadmap, product managers can ensure that the team is working efficiently and effectively to build an excellent product.

Prioritization:

Prioritization is a critical aspect of project management for product managers. By prioritizing work in the backlog, product managers can ensure that the team is working on the most important tasks first. Prioritization might involve considering factors like user impact, revenue potential, technical feasibility, or other criteria. By prioritizing work effectively, product managers can ensure that the team is making progress and delivering value to the business and the users.

Working with People and Stakeholders

As a product manager, you will need to work with a wide range of people and stakeholders to ensure the success of your product. This involves having effective communication skills, collaborating effectively with engineers and designers, and building relationships with executives and other stakeholders.

General Communication Skills

Effective communication is a critical skill for any product manager. You will need to communicate clearly and concisely with a wide range of people, including engineers, designers, executives, and other stakeholders. This means being able to express your ideas and requirements in a way that everyone can understand, and being able to listen actively to others to ensure you are fully aligned.

When communicating with others, be clear and direct, and avoid using jargon or technical terms that others may not understand. Use concrete examples and analogies to help explain complex concepts and be open to feedback and constructive criticism. Also, be sure to tailor your communication style to the person or group you are communicating with, considering their background, expertise, and communication preferences.

Working with Engineers: Collaborating effectively with engineers is a critical part of product management. Engineers are responsible for building the product, and you will need to work closely with them to ensure that the product meets the needs of your customers and stakeholders.

To work effectively with engineers, you will need to understand their technical capabilities and limitations, as well as their development process. This will help you communicate your requirements and priorities clearly and actionably. You should also be willing to listen to their input and feedback, as they will be able to provide valuable insights into the feasibility and complexity of your product ideas.

Additionally, it is important to establish a positive working relationship with your engineering team. This means building trust, showing respect for their expertise, and ensuring that they feel heard and valued.

Working with Designers

Designers are responsible for creating the user experience and interface for your product. As a product manager, you will need to work closely with them to ensure that the product meets the needs of your users and is easy to use.

To work effectively with designers, you will need to understand their design process and be able to provide clear and actionable feedback. This means having a deep understanding of your users' needs and preferences and being able to communicate those effectively to the design team.

It is also important to establish a positive working relationship with your design team. This means building trust, showing respect for their expertise, and ensuring that they feel heard and valued.

Working with Executives and Others

As a product manager, you will need to work with a wide range of stakeholders, including executives, marketing teams, sales teams, and customer support teams. These stakeholders will have different priorities and perspectives, and you will need to be able to communicate effectively with each of them to ensure that the product meets the needs of the business.

To work effectively with executives, you will need to understand their priorities and goals, and be able to communicate the value of your product in a way that resonates with them. This means focusing on the business outcomes that your product will enable, rather than just the features and functionality.

It is also important to establish a positive working relationship with executives and other stakeholders. This means building trust, showing respect for their expertise, and being responsive to their needs and concerns. Additionally, you should be willing to collaborate with them on defining the product strategy and roadmap and be open to feedback and constructive criticism.

What You Should Do to Prepare Yourself for the Job

Product management is a complex and demanding job that requires a wide range of skills and experience. To prepare yourself for the role, there are several steps you can take to build your expertise and demonstrate your potential-to-potential employers.

Get Relevant Experience

The first step to preparing yourself for a career in product management is to get relevant experience. This can include working in related fields such as marketing, engineering, or design, or taking on product management responsibilities in your current job.
One way to gain experience is to seek out internships or entry-level positions in product management at a company that interests you. This will give you exposure to the daily activities of a product manager and the opportunity to learn from experienced professionals in the field.
Another way to gain experience is to take on product management responsibilities in your current job, even if they are not officially part of your job description. For example, you could lead a cross-functional team to develop a new feature or work with your company's product manager to develop a new product.

Build a Portfolio with a Side Project

In addition to gaining experience, building a portfolio with a side project is a wonderful way to demonstrate your potential as a product manager. A side project can be anything from developing a mobile app to creating a website or designing a new product.
The key is to choose a project that allows you to highlight your skills and expertise in product management. This might include developing

a product roadmap, conducting market research, or working with a team to deliver a product to market.

When building your portfolio, be sure to document your process and the results of your project. This could include wireframes, user personas, and any other materials that demonstrate your approach to product management.

Brand Yourself

Finally, it is important to brand yourself as a product manager to stand out to potential employers. This means creating a professional presence on social media platforms such as LinkedIn, as well as building a personal website or blog.

When branding yourself, be sure to highlight your experience, skills, and achievements as a product manager. This might include case studies of successful product launches, recommendations from colleagues or mentors, and any industry publications or speaking engagements you have participated in.

It is also important to establish a personal brand that aligns with your career goals and values. This might include creating a unique brand voice or visual identity that sets you apart from other product managers in the field. Your personal brand should reflect your passion for product management and your commitment to delivering value to your customers and stakeholders.

How to Look for a Job in Product Management

Product management is a highly sought-after profession, and there are many job opportunities available for those looking to break into this field or advance their career. However, with so many options available, it can be overwhelming to know where to start. Here are some tips for how to look for a job in product management:

Where to look and what to look for

When looking for a job in product management, there are several places to start your search. Here are some options to consider:

- **Job boards:** Many job boards, such as LinkedIn, indeed, and Glassdoor, have dedicated sections for product management jobs. You can search by job title, location, and company size to find opportunities that fit your criteria.

- **Company websites:** Many companies will post their job openings on their own websites. This can be an effective way to find opportunities at companies you are interested in working for.

- **Networking:** Building relationships with people in the product management industry can be a wonderful way to learn about job openings before they are posted publicly. Attending industry events, connecting with people on LinkedIn, and joining product management groups to expand your network.

When looking for a job in product management, there are several things to consider in terms of the job itself. Look for a job that:

- **Aligns with your skills and interests:** Product management roles can vary widely in terms of the skills required and the industries they are in. Look for roles that align with your strengths and interests.

- **Offers opportunities for growth:** Look for a job that will challenge you and provide opportunities for growth and advancement.

- **Has a good company culture:** A positive work environment can be crucial to your success in a product management role. Look for a company with a culture that aligns with your values and priorities.

Inside advice on your PM job hunt

In addition to the above tips, there are some insider tips that can help you be more successful in your job search for a product management role:

- **Customize your resume and cover letter:** Tailor your resume and cover letter to the specific job you are applying for. Highlight your relevant skills and experiences and explain why you are a good fit for the role.

- **Prepare for the interview:** Research the company and the role ahead of time and prepare thoughtful questions to ask the interviewer. Practice answering common interview questions and be ready to give specific examples from your past experiences.

- **Highlight your problem-solving skills:** Product management is all about problem-solving, so be prepared to talk about how you have solved problems in your past roles. Provide specific examples of challenges you have faced and how you overcame them.

- **Show your passion for the industry:** Hiring managers want to see that you are passionate about product management and the industry. Be prepared to talk about why you are interested in the field and what motivates you.

By following these tips and advice, you can increase your chances of finding a fulfilling and rewarding job in product management.

How to Get a Job in Product Management

Product management is a highly competitive field, and getting the job requires a combination of experience, skills, and preparation. This section will provide tips on how to create a compelling resume, prepare for the product management interview, and answer interview questions in a way that impresses the hiring manager.

Resumes

Your resume is the first impression that a hiring manager will have of you, and it is essential that it is well-crafted and targeted to the specific product management role you are applying for. Here are some tips for creating a strong product management resume:

- **Highlight your experience:** List your product management experience at the top of your resume, including the products you have managed, the outcomes you have achieved, and the methodologies you have used.

- **Emphasize your skills:** Highlight your skills, including strategic thinking, leadership, problem-solving, data analysis, and communication.

- **Include relevant education:** If you have relevant education, such as an MBA, list it on your resume.

- **Use data to demonstrate your impact:** Include specific data points that demonstrate your impact on the products you have managed, such as revenue growth, user engagement, or customer satisfaction.

- **Tailor your resume to the job description:** Customize your resume to the specific product management job you are applying for, using keywords from the job description.

Interview for Product Management

The product management interview is designed to assess your experience, skills, and fit for the job. Here are some tips for preparing for the product management interview:

- **Research the company and the product:** Before the interview, research the company and the product you will be managing. This will help you to demonstrate your interest and knowledge during the interview.

- **Prepare examples of your work:** Prepare examples of your work that demonstrate your experience and skills, such as a product roadmap, a business case, or a product requirements document.

- **Practice your elevator pitch:** Prepare a 30-second elevator pitch that explains your experience, skills, and why you are interested in the product management role.

- **Be ready to answer frequent questions:** Be ready to answer common product management questions, such as "What is your product management philosophy?" and "How do you prioritize features?"

How to Answer Interview Questions the Right Way

Answering interview questions in a way that impresses the hiring manager is a key part of getting the product management job. Here are some tips for answering interview questions the right way:

- **Be specific:** Provide specific examples that demonstrate your experience and skills and use data to support your answers.

- **Be concise:** Keep your answers concise and to the point and avoid rambling or providing too much detail.

- **Demonstrate your thinking:** Demonstrate your thinking process and your approach to problem-solving, rather than just providing the answer.

- **Be honest:** Be honest about your experience and skills, and do not try to overstate your accomplishments.

Insider Tips for Getting the Job

Here are some insider tips for getting a product management job:

- **Build a network:** Build a network of product management professionals through industry events, online forums, and social media.

- **Get hands-on experience:** Gain hands-on experience by working on your own product ideas, participating in hackathons, or volunteering on open-source projects.

- **Focus on your soft skills:** Product management requires strong soft skills, such as leadership, communication, and collaboration. Focus on developing these skills through training, mentoring, or personal development.

- **Be persistent:** Getting the product management job can take time and persistence. Keep applying, practicing your interview skills, and building your network until you find the right opportunity.

After You've Got the Job the first things to do

Congratulations on getting your new product management job! Once you have landed the job, there are a few key things you should do to ensure you get off to a strong start and set yourself up for success. Here are some important steps to take:

Get to Know Your Team:

Your priority should be to get to know your team and build strong working relationships with them. Take the time to meet with each team member individually, learn about their backgrounds and areas of expertise, and understand their priorities and concerns. This will help you to build trust and establish a solid foundation for collaboration and teamwork.

Understand the Business:

It is important to understand the business and how your product fits into the larger picture. Take the time to learn about the company's history, mission, values, and strategy. Get to know the key stakeholders and decision-makers in the company and understand their priorities and goals. This will help you to make informed decisions and prioritize your product roadmap effectively.

Learn About the Product:

You should also spend time getting to know your product inside and out. Review all relevant documentation, such as product specs, user feedback, and customer support tickets. Meet with the engineering, design, and customer support teams to get a deep understanding of the product's technical capabilities, user experience, and customer needs. This will help you to identify areas for improvement and develop a product roadmap that addresses the most pressing needs of your customers.

Identify Key Metrics:

To measure the success of your product, you will need to identify the key metrics that matter. This might include user engagement, retention, revenue, or other relevant metrics. Work with your team and other stakeholders to identify the most important metrics for your product and develop a plan for how you will measure and track them over time. This will help you to make data-driven decisions and continuously improve your product over time.

Set Goals and Priorities:

Finally, you should set clear goals and priorities for your product. Based on your understanding of the business, the product, and the key metrics, identify the most key areas of focus for your product in the short and long term. Develop a product roadmap that outlines your priorities and goals, and work with your team to align everyone around these objectives. This will help you to stay focused and make progress towards your product's most important goals.

By taking these steps, you will be well on your way to building a successful product and establishing yourself as an effective product manager in your new role. Good luck!

Author Bio

Rathnakumar is a Tech professional with a diverse range of experiences and skills. His expertise is in the areas of data and AI, and he has worked with multiple Fortune 100 companies and high-growth startups in the data and AI space. In addition, he has been an entrepreneur for several years and has been a part of, having successfully launched, fundraised, and acquisitions of startups.

Aside from his work experience, Rathnakumar is also an author, blogger, YouTuber, Startup Mentor, and product manager. He is passionate about sharing his knowledge on a variety of topics, including entrepreneurship, technology, productivity, minimalism, startups, economics, and stocks. He uses a variety of mediums to share his insights, including books, blogs, and his YouTube channel.

If you want to learn more about Rathnakumar's work or connect with him, you can visit his website at www.rathnakumar.com. He is also active on social media, including LinkedIn, Facebook, Instagram, and Twitter, and is happy to connect.

Printed in Great Britain
by Amazon